MW00561443

OVERLOOKED CORNERS OF
EASTERN
NORTH
CAROLINA

RYAN STOWINSKY

AMERICA
THROUGH TIME®
ADDING COLOR TO AMERICAN HISTORY

America Through Time is an imprint of Fonthill Media LLC
www.through-time.com
office@through-time.com

Published by Arcadia Publishing by arrangement with Fonthill Media LLC
For all general information, please contact Arcadia Publishing:
Telephone: 843-853-2070
Fax: 843-853-0044
E-mail: sales@arcadiapublishing.com
For customer service and orders:
Toll-Free 1-888-313-2665

www.arcadiapublishing.com

First published 2022

Copyright © Ryan Stowinsky 2022

ISBN 978-1-63499-381-4

Typeset in Trade Gothic 10pt on 15pt
Printed and bound in England

CONTENTS

ABOUT THE AUTHOR

RYAN STOWINSKY has been visiting little-known historical sites, ghost towns, and other oddities in several states for over two decades. His website, stuofdoom.com, chronicles all the places he has visited. His writings and photographs have appeared in several books, newspapers, websites, and television shows. He graduated from Misericordia University in 2012 with a dual major in history and education. He currently resides in North Carolina with his wife and two daughters, where he teaches social studies.

INTRODUCTION

I compiled this book to share some of the lesser-known historical sites in Eastern North Carolina with anyone who is interested in the unusual. Although I have visited dozens of sites across the eastern half of this state, I wanted to select sites for this book that met a few criteria:

- They are historical. The sites must have some significance to Eastern North Carolina's history
- They are genuinely interesting. These are things people would actually want to go see; they make history entertaining or justify the effort to get to them
- They are free to visit. Short of gas and possibly tolls, none of these places charge an admission fee or require payment of any kind
- They are legal to visit. The places chosen are all on public or state-owned property
- They are little known. Virtually none of these places will be found in traditional travel books or any "Top 10 Things To Do" list; some are truly local secrets
- They are generally safe to visit. Most sites included in this book are in a park, found along a road, or require a short walk. Some will require a longer hike or access to a boat. This is discussed in their respective sections.

Basic directions to the sites are included in this book. My philosophy is simple: why read about a particular place if you can't go see it for yourself? Not to mention, directions for most of these sites are relatively easy to find online.

Some places in this collection are seldom visited or well off the beaten path. Because of this, I feel it is important to include the following pointers. If you are interested in visiting any of the harder to reach sites discussed in this book, please keep a few things in mind:

- Please do not take anything from these sites or damage them in any way. These sites are a part of everyone's history and should be preserved as best as possible. By taking artifacts, be it something you find in the woods or even a piece of a brick from a structure, you are not just stealing, but stealing history. As the tried-and-true saying goes, "Take nothing but pictures; leave nothing but footprints."
- Do not climb on or around old foundations. Many are centuries old and have loose bricks. By climbing on them, you risk damaging them; you could also fall and get hurt. Please do not vandalize any sites either; doing so could damage the site and hurts the site's historical integrity. Plus, it's just ugly and disrespectful.
- Don't trespass. Many places in the book border private property or otherwise have sections that are off limits. Some are off limits at nighttime or on holidays as well.
- GPS and mapping software are your friends. You pretty much can't get lost with them. It's also never a bad idea to waypoint your vehicle in an unfamiliar area.
- Wear appropriate footwear. Some sites require a bit of a walk to reach, and terrain can be sandy or rocky.
- Be prepared. Check the forecast before going. Bring an extra pair of shoes. Bring some water and a snack. Don't go alone. Let people know where you're going. Bring bug spray, especially if you are going out in summer. Bring sunscreen. Have emergency contacts in your phone in case your car breaks down or some other unexpected event unfolds. Know your limits and your vehicle's limits and stay safe.
- Give yourself plenty of daylight. In addition to many places closing or being off limits after dark, it can be dangerous to be out at night.
- Educate yourself on flora and fauna. Poison ivy, oak, and sumac can all be found in this part of the state. Mosquitoes, biting flies, no-see-ums, chiggers, and ticks are out there, especially in spring and summer months.

This list is not by any means meant to scare people off, but I want you to realize what could possibly happen if you don't adequately prepare. For a handful of these sites, you are literally going off the grid, so it's important to minimize risk. Have fun exploring, stay safe, and I hope you learn something while exploring Eastern North Carolina.

1

GHOST TOWNS AND ABANDONMENTS

W hether from changing industry, isolation, or forces of nature, many towns and settlements have come and gone in Eastern North Carolina. Some are no more than names on the map or piles of rubble, while others still contain foundations or other remnants of their former dwellings. Some simply outlived their purpose, while others never fully attained theirs. Many can be found in state or national parks and visitors can freely drive or walk up to them, while others involve some trekking. The following is a sampling of towns and abandoned sites from different time periods and regions of Eastern North Carolina.

RUINS FROM TWO ERAS: BRUNSWICK TOWN AND FORT ANDERSON

The historic site of Brunswick Town and Fort Anderson has the distinction of being home to ruins from two crucial points in American history—the Colonial era and the Civil War. Brunswick was settled in the 1720s and at the time was the major port of the Cape Fear region. The first successful British colonial town in the area, and also one of the largest for quite some time, Brunswick was home to two of North Carolina's colonial governors, Arthur Dobbs and William Tryon. The town earned a somewhat notorious reputation during the time of the Stamp Act, when armed citizens refused to allow ships carrying the infamous tax stamps to unload their cargo. Over the decades, however, nearby Wilmington built up and became a more desirable town, and people began to move there instead. The final blow came to the town in 1776 during the American Revolution, when British troops destroyed the town; due to the damage and the town's already dwindling population, it was never rebuilt.

Brunswick's story would not end there, however. Eighty-six years later, the Confederate Army decided it needed to boost its defenses around its now-crucial port town of Wilmington. Orders were given to build a fortress on the ruins of old Brunswick. Earthen mounds with guns, cannons, and bombproof shelters were constructed to slow down Union ships seen on the Cape Fear River. Materials from the old town were used in the fortifications.

Today, remains of both the Colonial-era town and the Civil War-era fortress can be visited on the site. The most prominent of the town's ruins is easily St. Philip's Church, an Anglican church and cemetery that was destroyed by the British during their raid in 1776. Today, its walls still stand. Foundations of many of Brunswick's buildings can be found along a walking path, with interpretive signs indicating the residents of each home. The trail eventually leads to the remaining earthworks of Fort Anderson. Also found in the area, a bit away from the rest of town, are the ruins of Russellborough, the mansion where the two royal governors resided.

Brunswick Town and Fort Anderson are state-run historical sites and are easy to reach. From Route 133, take Plantation Road to St. Philips Road; signs will also lead the way.

Outside and inside the walls of St. Philip's Church.

This plaque, placed by the Colonial Dames of America in 1902, discusses Brunswick's significance in defying the Stamp Act during the American Revolution. It can be found on the church ruins.

Some of the graves from the small cemetery next to St. Philip's.

BENJAMIN SMITH
SOLDIER AND STATESMAN
BORN
JAN.10,1756
DIED
JAN.10,1826
COLONEL IN REVOLUTIONARY ARMY
GOVERNOR OF NORTH CAROLINA
1811
GRAND MASTER OF MASONS
1808 - 1809 - 1810
THIS STONE PLACED BY THE
MASONS OF NORTH CAROLINA
1929

Remains of some of the home sites in Brunswick.

15

Earthen mounds and fortifications left over from the Civil War-era Fort Anderson.

Ruins at the site of the Russellborough, the mansion which housed two of North Carolina's royal governors.

AN UNREALIZED UTOPIA: SOUL CITY

During the 1960s, civil rights leader Floyd McKissick envisioned a brand new city that catered to minority groups and the impoverished. Originally meant to be for predominantly African Americans, the concept of Soul City was quickly opened to all races and backgrounds. With both private funding and assistance from the U.S. Department of Housing and Development, McKissick soon began building his utopia, named Soul City. He chose Warren County, North Carolina, for his site, partially due to the area's poverty and high school dropout rate; ideally, this "city of all races" would create jobs, increase the local population, and help turn things around economically and culturally for people in the area. McKissick built an industrial building, Soultech I, so that factory jobs would be readily available in town for the people he hoped to attract.

Unfortunately, the dream barely took off. People were hesitant to move to an experimental city in an impoverished area; Soul City's population was in the double digits for much of its early history. Then in 1973, Soul City was accused of corruption, nepotism, and other charges. Although the federal government cleared the town of all charges two years later, these accusations, combined with the stagnant population, sealed the fate of Soul City; it would never have the influx of people and companies bringing in jobs. Floyd McKissick never gave up on his dream, however, and continued to promote the town and lived there until his death in 1991; he is buried in a small cemetery in town.

Today, the population of Soul City hovers around 1,000, but the self-sufficient community visualized by McKissick is nowhere to be found. Many planned streets lined with only streetlights can be found just outside the central "hub" of town, while others simply dead end or are blocked off by trees or debris. Several businesses, including many medical services, are vacant. Soultech I, which never accomplished its intended purpose, was purchased by the county prison. The town's park, originally managed by the town itself, has also been taken over by the county.

A large sign once greeted drivers along Route 1, but this has since been moved to the heart of town. With the easily identifiable landmark gone, most drivers are unaware they are driving past a social experiment. To reach Soul City from Route 1, simply turn onto Soul City Boulevard and take it until the end. To see the unique sign and the central hub, turn left on Manson-Axtell Road, then left again on Liberation Road; look for the large Soul City sign on your left.

A large sign for Soul City once sat alongside Route 1. It has since been moved to the front of the center of town. Today, a normal street sign is the only indicator of the town from the highway.

One of many roads in Soul City that goes nowhere.

Only streetlights line some of the roads outside the center of town. Planned developments remain unfinished.

Some roads have been barricaded, making them impassable.

One of many abandoned buildings found on the outskirts of Soul City.

Inside one of the abandonments.

Some of the original wooden street signs remain but are in bad shape.

Some ruins found in the woods near the park in Soul City.

Floyd McCissick, founder of Soul City, is buried in a small cemetery in town.

COLD WAR RELICS: TOPSAIL'S ISLAND'S COLD WAR TOWERS

Topsail Island may be a popular tourist destination today, but just a few decades ago, it was an unpopulated barrier island, with the only visitors being occasional fishermen. Due to its isolation, the United States Navy eyed it as a test site for what was dubbed Operation Bumblebee. This top-secret operation allowed the military to develop and test surface-to-air missiles. An assembly building and eight observation towers were constructed on the island, most of which still survive today. In a course of less than two years, from 1946 until 1948, roughly 200 missiles were built and fired.

Seven of the eight towers still stand, though most are now privately owned or have even been incorporated into homes or condos; the northernmost tower, Tower 8, was demolished in the late 1980s, due to trespassers falling to their deaths after entering it. The assembly building now serves as a museum recording the island's military history and is easy to spot with the full-sized Talos missile mounted outside. The towers stretch along much of the shorelines of Surf City and Topsail Beach and can be found both seaside and bayside. Probably the most well known and most visited of all the towers is Tower 3, which sits on the beach right at the border of North Topsail Beach and Surf City. Though visitors can walk right up to it, the interior of the tower is off limits.

The remaining towers can be found at various locations on Topsail Island. Maps giving the locations of all the sites significant to Operation Bumblebee can easily be found online. Keep in mind that other than the assembly building museum, all are privately owned or otherwise off limits.

Tower 3 is right on the beach, between the towns of Surf City and North Topsail.

Various angles of Tower 3.

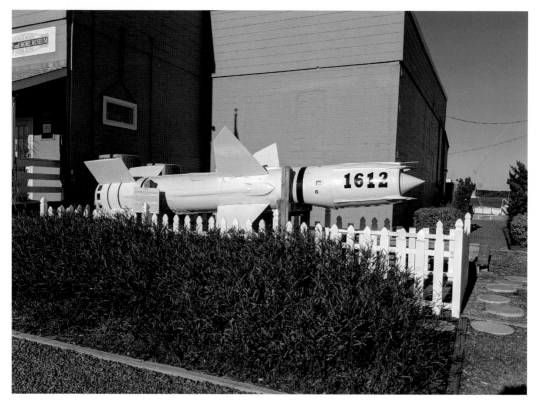

A Talos missile sits outside the old assembly building, now a museum.

Some of the towers have been converted into private homes or incorporated into other buildings.

Another tower found farther up the island. Construction made it unreachable.

CUT OFF FROM THE REST OF THE WORLD: LONELY PORTSMOUTH

Few places in North Carolina are as remote as the ghost town of Portsmouth. The former town, all alone on a 13-mile-long, uninhabited island, is difficult to reach. It is accessible only by private ferries out of Atlantic Beach and Ocracoke Island, both of which are also quite out of the way for most. Other than the occasional visitor, National Park volunteer, or fisherman, Portsmouth and its several houses and church remain empty most of the time, though a homecoming is held there every other year.

In the colonial days, Portsmouth was a bustling port town, servicing hundreds of ships a year. By its peak in the mid-1800s, Portsmouth's population was approximately 500 to 700, with several churches and businesses in town. However, once the Hatteras and Oregon Inlets were opened up in the 1860s, industry moved farther up the Outer Banks, and the town quickly began to lose its luster. It is no surprise that the Outer Banks are prone to hurricanes, and these storms also had some say in the decline of the town. Ocracoke Inlet became narrower and shallower, especially after a fierce hurricane in 1846, making it increasingly difficult for ships to pass. With the newer inlets being safer and more accessible, businesses and people began to leave.

By 1955, only twelve residents lived on the island permanently; by 1971, that number was reduced to three. Henry Pigott, the last man to live on the island, passed away in January of 1971. Shortly afterward, the final two inhabitants, Marion Babb and Elma Dixon, left the island and moved to Beaufort, though they did continue to visit their former homes for a time. At this point, the National Park Service took charge of the village and remains in control of it today.

Roughly a dozen buildings still remain in Portsmouth, including a general store, a Methodist church, and a one-room schoolhouse. Some buildings can be entered, but most remain off limits to visitors. Several small cemeteries are scattered about the village, including that of a man who was mistaken for John Wilkes Booth shortly after the assassination of President Lincoln. A few interpretive signs can be found outside some of the buildings, including Henry Pigott's former dwelling. There are no paved roads in Portsmouth, only dirt pathways. Biting flies and mosquitoes are unavoidable, and if one strays too far from the center of the village, unbearable. Ibises crowd in some of the dead, windswept trees, with nobody around to disturb them. The only indication of outside intervention is the grass being cut by National Park Services volunteers.

Due to its isolation, Portsmouth offers no modern conveniences, save for restrooms in the makeshift National Park Service office. There is no fresh water or food. Visitors must bring in what they will need for their trip.

While technically free to visit, reaching Portsmouth is not an easy task if one does not have access to a boat. Only a handful of private ferries run to the town, and only for part of the year—usually about March until September or October. As of this writing, only one company offers tours to Portsmouth from Atlantic Beach, and it is roughly a one-hour voyage. Most visitors come from Ocracoke, which is only about a 20-minute ride to Portsmouth. None of the companies currently offer online reservations and must be called ahead of time. They also only take cash. The author strongly recommends Portsmouth Island Boat Tours, out of Ocracoke. Plan ahead, as tours fill up very quickly in summer months. Sunblock, water, food, and DEET bug spray are strongly recommended.

A dirt path leads from the dock to town.

The former home of Theodore and Annie Salter now serves as a visitor center and office for the National Parks Service.

Most of the surviving buildings are in good condition but show obvious signs of wear from the elements.

Some of the buildings can be entered by visitors.

Exterior and interior of the general store.

Despite its size, the village of Portsmouth is
surprisingly spread out.

Several small cemeteries dot Portsmouth.

Former home of Henry Pigott, the last man to live permanently in Portsmouth. Shortly after his death, the final two inhabitants left.

Exterior and interior of the Methodist church, the only remaining church on the island.

Ibises congregate in a dead tree in front of Portsmouth's one-room schoolhouse.

"HE MADE PEOPLE THINK": THE BUNKER AND GRAVE OF THE FORT FISHER HERMIT

Fort Fisher State Recreation Area, south of Wilmington, is a popular tourist destination with lots to see and do. For history buffs, the remains of its Civil War-era fortress can be toured. Lovers of the outdoors can enjoy fishing, walking on the beach, and hiking. One of the state's aquariums is even located there. Most visitors, however, are not aware that Fort Fisher has an interesting little bit of history that until recently remained largely unknown to outsiders; an abandoned World War II bunker in the park was once home to a hermit.

Back in 1955, sixty-two-year-old Robert Harrill decided he had had enough of civilization and hitchhiked over 250 miles to Fort Fisher. After getting sent back once for vagrancy, he returned a year later and settled in an empty bunker he found south of Fort Fisher. Robert learned to live off the land and grew a vegetable garden near his new home. Over time, he became quite the local celebrity, with thousands of people visiting him during his fifteen-year stay at his bunker. He would discuss philosophy and other deep topics with anyone who came out to visit him.

Sadly, in 1972, Robert was found dead in his bunker, with several wounds on his body. His death remains a mystery, with some claiming he was murdered because he attempted to claim squatters' rights on this portion of Fort Fisher. Some believe teenagers attacked him at night, and that his death was a prank gone horribly wrong. Despite being wounded and covered in blood and sand, the official cause of death was recorded as a heart attack. Robert was buried in Newton Cemetery in Carolina Beach. His grave is lined with stones and shells and is adorned with trinkets and small figurines from visitors. His headstone reads: "He made people think."

To reach the Fort Fisher Hermit's bunker, drive down Route 421 from Wilmington (alternately, take the ferry from Southport). Park in the public beach access parking lot and look for signs for the Basin Trail. The trail is just over a mile and crosses through maritime forest, beach, and salt marsh. The bunker is found along the trail. Robert's grave is just a few miles away on Dow Road (it runs parallel to 421 for a while). Look for the sign for Federal Point Methodist Church Cemetery. Park in the pull-off and walk down the trail a bit. Robert's grave can be found in the adjacent Newton Cemetery (which has quite a history of its own; make sure to read the signage). Not surprisingly, his grave is often the most decorated, making it easy to find.

The bunker is a few yards off the Basin Trail. A small pathway leads to it.

The bunker, Robert Harrill's home for years.

Robert E. Harrill
"The Fort Fisher Hermit"

CALLED THIS DESERTED WWII BUNKER
HOME FROM 1956 - 1972. HE ATTRACTED
THOUSANDS WHO SHARED HIS VIEWS OF
SOCIETY, GOVERNMENT AND THE NEED OF
"COMMON SENSE." HIS BODY WAS FOUND
THE MORNING OF JUNE 4, 1972. HIS
DEATH IS UNSOLVED (YET). HIS GRAVE
IS AT THE FEDERAL POINT CEMETERY.
THE HERMIT SOCIETY 1995

A small plaque placed on the front of the bunker pays homage to Mr. Harrill.

Inside the small, one-room bunker.

Above: Other remnants from the bunker's WWII days can be seen in the marsh directly behind it.

Left: Harrill's grave can be found farther north on the island, in the Federal Point Methodist Church cemetery.

2

UNIQUE GRAVES AND CEMETERIES

For centuries, settlements and industries have come and gone in Eastern North Carolina, and naturally their people came and went with them. Early settlers lived and worked their entire lives there, and even though many of the old towns and homesteads no longer remain, graves of some of their people do. In some cases, people did unusual things to honor their dead, while in other cases, the modern world struggled with preserving these places of rest while attempting to use the land for commercial purposes. The following is a collection of some of the more unique graves and cemeteries found in Eastern North Carolina.

IF YOU ARE A FRIEND, CAST A STONE: THE GRAVE OF NATHANIEL MACON

Just north of the town of Vaughan is an unusual site—a small family cemetery with each grave covered with piles of stones. This is no act of vandalism, however; the interred, very important to the early history of both North Carolina and the United States as a whole, requested stones be placed on his grave. Centuries later, visitors still abide.

Nathaniel Macon served as a congressman for the early United States for decades, holding both Speaker of the House and President Pro Tempore of the Senate during his extensive career. An anti-Federalist, Macon initially opposed the ratification of the Constitution. He and other anti-Federalists worried that a strong central government could become too powerful and control the lives of citizens of the young and vulnerable United States; this concern helped lead to the creation of the Bill of

Rights to further protect the rights of Americans. Thomas Jefferson, good friends with Macon, referred to him as the "Last of the Romans," reflecting his passion for individual liberty and disapproval of oppressive government.

When Macon died in 1837, he left enough money for his funeral to provide "dinner and grog" for about 1,500 guests. He requested each friend place a stone on his grave, and they obliged. Over the decades, however, several "friends" have placed rocks on Macon's grave site. His wife and son, who both passed on decades before him, are also buried here and have their own piles of stones as well.

The grave of Nathaniel Macon can be found off Route 158. Turn onto Eaton Ferry Road and look for signs leading to the senator's grave. Turn on to Nathaniel Macon Drive. The cemetery will be on the right; just look for the large piles of rocks. Across from the cemetery are some historic buildings from Macon's former plantation, Buck Spring. His actual home burned down in 1977, but a replica has been built on the site. An original smokehouse and corn crib still stand.

The graves of Nathaniel Macon and his immediate family. Over two centuries' worth of stones are piled on them.

Unsurprisingly, Nathaniel's grave has the largest pile of stones.

Close-up of Nathaniel's stone.

A few signs lead curiosity seekers to the Macon gravesite.

Some of Macon's homestead is preserved, including a replica of his house and a corn crib.

ETERNAL REST IN THE MALL PARKING LOT: THE EVANS FAMILY CEMETERY

When it comes to land, sometimes the past and present conflict. One such example can be found in the parking lot of the Greenville Mall. Visitors to the mall may notice a small brick enclosure just in front of the main entrance. To most people, it appears as an unimpressive, empty structure, with its walls just tall enough to hide its contents from view. Upon closer inspection, however, it becomes clear that the wall is concealing a graveyard. No interpretive signs can be found; instead, a single plaque on the rear wall simply reads, "Evans Family Cemetery." A small gate on the front wall is the only entrance and break in the wall, which is likely why the majority of mall goers are unaware of its existence; from most angles, it is literally just out of view.

Interestingly, the entire grounds of the cemetery have been paved over with asphalt and brick. The graves range from the mid-1800s to the early 1900s. While a handful of graves are intact, most of the headstones are broken and lie on the ground. A few have illegible dates. Garbage litters the ground inside the cemetery's walls, and weeds grow through the cracks in the pavement. It is clear little care has been given to this site recently.

The Evans Family Cemetery can easily be found just in front of the main entrance of the Greenville Mall, just behind the Carolina Ale House. Just look for the brick walls.

The cemetery is just in front of the mall's main entrance, enclosed by a brick wall.

IN MEMORY OF
JOHN S. EVANS AND HIS WIFE
BORN IN FRONTIER DAYS OF 18th CENTURY.
DIED IN 19th CENTURY PRIOR TO 1858.
WERE PARENTS OF CORNELIA (1814),
JOHN (1815), RICHARD (1816), NANCY (1817),
ABNER (1819), ELIZABETH (1826),
ALL BURIED HEREIN, AND FIVE OTHER CHILDREN BURIED ELSEWHERE

This stone gives some background to the Evans family.

Most of the stones are broken and lie next to their bases.

Above left: One of the few gravestones still standing.

Above right: The gate to the cemetery.

Right: This small plaque on the outer rear wall is the only indicator of the cemetery.

A Promise is a Promise: The "Rum Keg Girl" and Other Curiosities of the Old Burying Ground

Beaufort, one of North Carolina's oldest towns, is home to the Old Burying Ground, a centuries-old cemetery that acts as a chronicle to the history of both North Carolina and the United States. Veterans from several wars, including the Revolution, the War of 1812, and the Civil War, can be found interred here. Many graves were originally marked with wood, shell, or brick. Time has caused many of the oldest markers to crumble or rot away. Although many interesting graves can be found in this small and erratic cemetery, the grave of the "Rum Keg Girl" is easily what draws most curiosity seekers.

Her name has been lost to time, but the story of the girl is still remembered. Her parents came to North Carolina from England during the Colonial era, and as she got older she heard stories of her homeland and begged her family to visit England. Once she was older (estimates say from ten to twelve years old), her father, who was a sea merchant, agreed to take her to England. The girl's mother, worried about the weeks-long journey at sea, made her husband promise to bring their daughter back.

The father and daughter enjoyed their trip to England, but during the voyage back, the girl died for some unidentified reason. Because the journey across the Atlantic took weeks to complete back then, people who died on the voyage tended to be buried at sea; however, the father had promised to bring the girl back home. So, the story goes, he bought a barrel of rum from the ship's captain and placed his daughter's body inside. Once they returned to North Carolina, the entire keg was buried in the cemetery. The frail, wooden grave marker is barely legible, and it simply states, "Little Girl Buried in Rum Keg." Visitors regularly cover the girl's grave in toys, shells, stuffed animals, and other trinkets. In 2016, a vandal set fire to the grave. Though damaged, the old, wooden marker survived the fire.

The Rum Keg Girl is just one of several points of interest in Old Burying Ground. A British officer was buried "standing in salute to his Majesty King George III," according to the sign by his otherwise unmarked grave. Captain Otway Burns, an American privateer during the War of 1812, has one of the cannons from his ship, *The Snap Dragon*, mounted on his tomb. The rear left corner of the cemetery looks empty, but a sign indicates that many settlers killed during the Tuscarora Indian War of 1711 are buried there.

The Old Burying Ground is found at 400 Ann Street in Beaufort and is open daily from 9:30 am until 5 pm. Maps offering a guided tour of the more unique sites in the cemetery can be found just inside the gate.

The wooden grave marker of the anonymous "Rum Barrel Girl."

Visitors decorate the grave of the "Rum Barrel Girl" with toys, flowers, shells, and trinkets.

Gravesite of a British troop, buried standing and saluting King George III.

Grave of Captain Otway Burns, American privateer during the War of 1812. One of the cannons from his ship, *The Snap Dragon*, adorns his stone.

here lies the remains of
the settlers killed during
the Tuscarora Indian War
September 1711

Mass grave of settlers killed during Tuscarora War, a conflict between the Tuscarora tribe and British colonists.

Different sections of the cemetery. Some parts are in good condition or have been maintained, while others have fallen badly into disrepair.

A CEMETERY AND AN ARBORETUM: TARBORO'S CALVARY EPISCOPAL CHURCH GROUNDS

Rector Joseph Blount Cheshire was both a devout man and an ardent botanist who, in the mid-1800s, came up with a creative way to not only blend his two passions but to also beautify his church grounds and boost attendance: he had both native and exotic flora planted at his churches, among the graves. Although Cheshire had plants sent to all the churches where he preached, by far his best-known work is at the Calvary Episcopal Church in Tarboro, often listed as one of North Carolina's greatest arboretums.

Visitors to the church today are greeted by a garden-like setting, with signs among the headstones, as well as attached to trees, identifying the species of plants. Ivy covers much of the ground and creeps up many of the graves and trees, some of which were planted by Cheshire himself. With the church grounds enclosed by brick walls, it feels almost like walking into a secret garden. A century-and-a-half later, Cheshire's work still shines, with many of the bushes and trees towering over the graves and lining the pathways through the cemetery.

Of course, some of the stones have their own stories to tell. The grave of the youngest major general of the Confederate Army to be killed in battle, William Dorsey Pender, is located here; his grave is easy to spot since it is lined with cannonballs. Another grave is a sad reminder of two best friends who lost their lives together in a swimming accident; their shared stone plainly gives their first names and says, "Accidentally drowned." Several clergy members, a former North Carolina governor, and even Cheshire's son are also interred here.

The grounds of the Calvary Episcopal Church are open to the public most days. The church can be found in downtown Tarboro on East Church Road.

Entering the grounds is almost otherworldly.

Above left: Shared gravestone of two friends who drowned in the same accident.

Above right: One of the tags used to identify the plants in the arboretum/cemetery.

Above: Grave of Confederate Major General William Dorsey Pender, the youngest of his rank to be killed in the Civil War. He died at Gettysburg.

Right: Looking down the outdoor corridor.

Some stones are quite simplistic with their epitaphs.

Various photos from the grounds. The cemetery and the flora complement each other perfectly, and the plants do not overtake the stones. Paths are clear and well maintained.

Honoring Our Allies: The British Cemeteries of the Outer Banks

Although the United States entered World War II after the attack on Pearl Harbor in December of 1941, it needed time to draft, train, and equip men for all branches of its military. As it was doing so, its long-time ally Great Britain loaned the then-vulnerable United States some of its naval power, since German U-boats freely patrolled the Atlantic Ocean and had been known to attack ships off the eastern coast of the US.

One such British ship, the HMT *Bedfordshire*, was torpedoed by a U-boat in May of 1942. The thirty-seven crew members aboard all perished, and four of the men from this tragedy washed up on Ocracoke shortly afterward, with two never being identified. Due to Ocracoke's isolation at the time, as well as the threat of more U-boats, it was decided that the recovered British service members would be buried on Ocracoke rather than transported back home. The cemetery is permanently leased to Great Britain, meaning that technically the land within the cemetery's perimeter is British.

A smaller and lesser-known cemetery interring two men from the British Navy can be found on Hatteras Island, just down the road from the Cape Hatteras Lighthouse. Just a few weeks before the sinking of the HMT *Bedfordshire*, a British tanker, the *San Delfino*, was hit by torpedoes seven times off the coast of Hatteras. Of the fifty aboard, twenty-eight perished. Shortly afterward, one of the *San Delfino's* crew washed ashore; a second unidentified man would follow suit two weeks later, leading some to speculate that he was possibly from the sinking at Ocracoke just days before.

Memorial services are held at both British cemeteries annually, near the dates of the tragedies. The cemetery on Ocracoke is cared for by the Ocracoke Coast Guard Station, while the one on Hatteras is maintained by the Commonwealth War Graves Commission and the National Park Service.

The British cemetery on Ocracoke is fairly easy to find; however, getting onto Ocracoke Island itself requires a boat, private plane, or ferry (the State provides free ferry service from Hatteras and paid service from Cedar Island). Once in the town of Ocracoke, simply turn onto British Cemetery Road and follow it until arriving at the island's main cemetery. The British graves are sectioned off in their own plot. To reach the cemetery on Hatteras, turn onto Lighthouse Road off Route 12 in Buxton. Past the lighthouse area, signs lead visitors to the cemetery. Please keep in mind that entry into the actual cemetery perimeters is prohibited.

The British cemetery on Ocracoke is separate from the main cemetery. Its interior is technically British territory.

Memorial to all those lost on the HMT *Bedfordshire*.

HMT BEDFORDSHIRE

AN ARCTIC TRAWLER, BUILT IN 1935 BY SMITH'S DOCK CO. OF MIDDLEBROUGH, ENGLAND. IN 1939 SOLD TO THE ADMIRALTY AND CONVERTED TO AN ARMED TRAWLER. IN 1942 IT WAS ONE OF THE 24 TRAWLERS LOANED TO THE U.S. NAVY FOR COASTAL PATROL. ARMAMENT; ONE 4" GUN, ONE MACHINE GUN AND DEPTH CHARGES.

An etching on the corner of the memorial shows what the ship looked like.

Short poem mounted at the site.

Stone for one of the unidentified men buried here.

The British naval flag flies over the cemetery.

The British cemetery found on Hatteras Island, not too far from the Cape Hatteras Lighthouse.

Close-ups of the two Hatteras stones.

The Hatteras British cemetery is just a short walk down a path.

3

ODDS AND ENDS: MORE UNIQUE AND HISTORICAL SITES

E astern North Carolina is full of lesser-known historical sites and roadside stops, ranging from the bizarre to the tragic to the enlightening. A few are only known to locals, while others are overlooked or difficult to reach. For some, they may be a roadside oddity that people simply pass by while asking, "What on earth was that?" without understanding just why it is there. The following is an assortment of some sites that are difficult to categorize but are still worth a visit.

THE HIGHWAY GOES UNDER THE LAKE: OLD HIGHWAY 98

At first glance, Forest Ridge Park in Wake Forest looks like any regular park, with a large playground, hiking trails, and fishing spots. Many are not aware, however, that the main road leading into the park was once an old highway, and evidence of this can still be found along the park's main trail. What many mistake for an unmaintained boat ramp is actually the old road going directly into Falls Lake.

In the late 1970s and early 1980s, the U.S. Army Corps of Engineers was tasked with creating reservoirs to help with North Carolina's growing population and to also help control the flooding of the Neuse River, and Falls Lake was one of these man-made bodies of water. Unfortunately, this required the government to claim eminent domain on much of the surrounding land where the new reservoirs would lie. Many families and businesses lost their properties and were forced to relocate. These properties and the roads that led to them became abandoned. While the buildings were often demolished, the roads were largely ignored and left as they were.

Today, remnants of Old Highway and some old properties can be found along the trails of Forest Ridge Park. The main trail that leads to the lake is actually the old highway, and if visitors look carefully, they can see the median and shoulder lines are still on the old road. Just off the path along the Old Highway 98 Trail and the Peninsula Trail, foundations and remnants of some of the old home sites are still fairly easy to find.

Forest Ridge Park is easily found at the very end of Old Highway 98 in Wake Forest, which in turn can be accessed from Old Falls of Neuse Road. A gate forces vehicles to go to the parking area to the left; the remains of Old Highway 98, as well as the trails, are just past this gate.

Old Highway 98 goes straight into Falls Lake in Forest Ridge Park.

Old Highway 98's median and shoulder lines are still visible in spots.

Ruins from some of the claimed homes found just off the trails.

No Postage Required: The Kindred Spirit Mailbox

Sitting just a few hundred yards from the South Carolina border, tucked slightly behind a dune on an empty stretch of beach, is what some dub North Carolina's loneliest mailbox: the Kindred Spirit Mailbox. This local treasure has only in recent years become more widely known, due to its uniqueness and effort required to get to it. For years, people have walked to nearly the end of the island of Sunset Beach to write letters to total strangers or to read other travelers' words left in the mailbox. Some letters are words of encouragement, while some discuss hardships people have endured; one can never be sure what is in store for them when opening the Kindred Spirit. In addition to the exchanging of anonymous letters, the site is also becoming a popular spot for weddings and vow renewals. In recent years, the Kindred Spirit Mailbox has even been the subject of a few novels.

The closest parking to the mailbox is nearly 1.5 miles away, so the mailbox is not visited very frequently. For those who do make the trek, a pleasant walk along an undeveloped and unspoiled beach awaits them. A flagpole with an American flag behind a dune gives away the location of the mailbox. A small bench next to the mailbox provides a place to rest, enjoy the views, and read others' letters or write a letter of one's own in the multiple notebooks left inside the mailbox. Not far past the mailbox, on the South Carolina side of the border, is a jetty jutting out into the ocean that visitors can walk.

Throughout its history, the mailbox has been damaged, knocked over, and even blown away by hurricanes. Volunteers have repaired or replaced it each time; a recent site repair actually made the front page of a local newspaper. These kindred spirits also make sure there are empty notebooks in the mailbox and take away the full ones, and many of these full notebooks have been displayed in local museums and university libraries.

Getting to the Kindred Spirit Mailbox is straightforward but requires a hike. Take Sunset Boulevard, the only road to and from Sunset Beach. For closest possible parking, turn right on North Shore Drive West. Take it to the end, to 40th Street. This is the closest public parking and beach access; however, there are only a handful of spots, and even from here, it is nearly a 1.5-mile walk to the mailbox. The island's main parking lot and beach access can be found at the intersection of Sunset Boulevard and North Shore Drive, but this will add significant distance to the walk. Once on the beach, just walk southwest toward the mailbox and look for a flagpole.

Even from the closest parking, the walk to the mailbox and back is nearly three miles.

The Kindred Spirit Mailbox.

The mailbox contains notebooks, in which visitors write their letters.

People resting and writing or reading letters from inside the mailbox.

The trek to and from the mailbox is mostly empty beach.

Annie Went Home: The Empty Grave of Annie Lee

Just south of Warrenton can be found a grave site with an unusual and tragic story. The grave in question is that of Anne Carter "Annie" Lee, daughter of none other than General Robert E. Lee. Even more interesting is the fact that the grave is now empty and has been for quite some time.

Shortly after the Civil War broke out, the family of General Robert E. Lee vacated their family estate in Arlington, Virginia, to avoid being captured by Union troops. Although they briefly stayed with a family member elsewhere in Virginia, the Lees eventually crossed into North Carolina and stayed at Jones Springs, one of several sulfur springs resorts that once drew visitors to the region. In 1862, Annie contracted typhoid and died shortly afterward. The Lee family was in a predicament; they could not return to Arlington to bury Annie, since home was now behind enemy lines. The Jones family offered to allow Annie to be buried in their own family plot. A local stone cutter and Confederate soldier, Zerald Crowder, carved the 11-foot obelisk that marks her grave. In 1870, Robert E. Lee himself visited the grave of his daughter and gave it his blessing. He died shortly afterward.

What was supposed to be the final resting place for General Lee's daughter became a target for vandalism in the twentieth century. A historical sign placed by the state along a nearby main road was cut down and thrown in a ditch. In 1994, vandals toppled Annie Lee's pillar, leading to her modern-day descendants requesting her remains be moved to the family crypt. After over 130 years, Annie was reunited with her family and interred at Lee Chapel, which is on the grounds of Washington & Lee University in Lexington, Virginia. Her original grave marker, however, remains where it was originally erected.

The vacant grave of Annie Lee can be found just off Route 401, a few miles south of Warrenton. Turn onto Annie Lee Road and look for the cemetery on the left.

The empty grave of Annie Lee is in the corner of the cemetery.

Annie Lee's stone is becoming difficult to read.

The small cemetery that formerly interred Annie Lee. Nothing at the site indicates that she was exhumed and moved to Virginia.

UFO IN THE OUTER BANKS: NORTH CAROLINA'S LONE HOUSE OF THE FUTURE

In the 1960s, Finnish designer Matti Suuronen designed what he hoped would be seen as "the house of the future"—the Futuro House. Reflecting the science fiction movies and Space Age mentality from the time, these homes were shaped like the archetypal "flying saucer" UFO, with several round windows and even a hatch instead of a traditional doorway. The homes were made of fiberglass-reinforced polyester plastic and were designed to be portable; Surronen's original vision for these homes was for them to be movable ski cabins that would be quick to heat.

Despite being manufactured at the height of the Space Race, these kitschy houses never really caught on, and it is estimated that fewer than one hundred were ever sold. The Oil Crisis of 1973 did not help the struggling Futuro homes either, causing the price of the plastic used to build them to triple. Production of the homes quickly ceased, and very few were used for their actual purposes; over the years most have simply become collectors' pieces, while several have been demolished. Just a few decades later, only roughly half of the known Futuros survive; though they are distributed throughout the world, just a single one of these homes can be found in North Carolina, near the bottom of Hatteras Island.

In the town of Frisco at the bottom of Hatteras Island, the shiny, metallic UFO greets beach goers traveling along Route 12. Aliens, stickers, action figures, and other oddities greet visitors from the home's windows, steps, and grounds. The house has lived many lives, including a meeting place for scouts and a hot dog stand. Today, it is simply a roadside attraction to ponder. Although on private property, travelers are welcome to stop, and a small parking area is even provided for those curious enough to stop.

The Futuro House is hard to miss. Just look for the UFO on Route 12, near mile marker 66 in Frisco.

The Futuro House of Frisco, the only remaining Futuro House in all of North Carolina. Nearly each window has some sort of creature displayed.

The hatch is open, with stairs leading up to the UFO's door.

Inside the stairway. The UFO cannot be entered.

Various things, including a boat, action figures, and a moped, are found around the outside of the Futuro House's lot.

BIBLIOGRAPHY

Books

Calkins, Carroll C. (Ed.) *Off the Beaten Path.* The Reader's Digest Association, 1987.
Crouch. A. L. *The Kindred Letters.* Published by the author, 2019.
Lefler, Hugh T. *North Carolina History.* University of North Carolina Press, 1934.
Price, William S. *Nathaniel Macon of North Carolina—Three Views of His Character and Creed.* University of North Carolina Press, 2008.

Websites

beauforthistoricsite.org/old-burying-ground/
findagrave.com
geocaching.com
ghosttowns.com
historicsites.nc.gov
ncdcr.gov
ncpedia.org
northcarolinaghosts.com
northcarolinahistory.org
thefuturohouse.com
warrenrecord.com